Quotes and Phrases that Inspire Productivity and Sales

60 power-quotes from the Sales Leader and Best Selling Author Anthony Camacho!

It is time to take your sales and business into your own hands and create a culture of successful and positive sales professionals. Shift the outlook of your team in a more powerful and thriving way.

In this Amazing Itty Bitty® Book, "Hitman", Anthony Camacho uses inspirational quotes to assist in removing the plague of negativity from your daily sales along with your daily life.

Who will benefit from this book: Sales professionals, Business Leaders, Entrepreneurs, and so many more.

Have a new impact on your sales with mental toughness by reading this book cover-to-cover, reading and reflecting on one quote per day or week, or by focusing on a specific topic, i.e. cold calling, follow-up, etc.

"Build strong affirmations for a successful day. Live by COURAGE, STRENGTH, and AMBITION IN SALES. ~Anthony Camacho

Pick up this Amazing Itty Bitty® Book today to learn and be motivated by the sales Master!

Your Amazing Itty Bitty® Little Black Book of Sales Quotes

60 Powerful Phrases Designed to Empower Your Entrepreneurial Mind

Anthony Camacho

Published by Itty Bitty® Publishing
A subsidiary of S & P Productions, Inc.

Copyright © 2017 Anthony Camacho

Printed in the United States of America

Itty Bitty® Publishing
311 Main Street, Suite D
El Segundo, CA 90245
(310) 640-8885

ISBN: 978-0-9992211-7-4

Dedication

I would like to dedicate this book to the following Mentors and Great Leaders who have inspired me positively and powerfully. I greatly appreciate your time and most importantly your friendship. I thank each of you for the way you have contributed to my success on this Professional and Spiritual journey of life. Thank you for making this world a better place for your family, friends, employees and customers.

- Richard Romero, General Manager Hollywood, Toyota
- Michael Gay, Service Director Metro Nissan
- Paul Cummings, CEO Paul Cummings Enterprises
- Richard Garcia, Grand Master Kenpo Martial Arts
- Sandra Ayala, Catholic Spiritual Director/Advisor
- Richard Bonar, Franchisee Dale Carnegie Training
- Andrew Arizmendi, General Manager Rusnak Bentley, Rolls-Royce
- Nick Cardin, Vice President Puente Hills Toyota
- Daniel Charlier, EVC Financial Advisor WFG
- John Rost, CEO Fiesta Franchise Corporation
- Bill Walsh, CEO/Founder Power Team USA

Stop by our Itty Bitty® website to find interesting information regarding Sales and Business.

www.IttyBittyPublishing.com

Or visit Anthony Camacho at
http://www.topproducerfactory.com/

Table of Contents

INTRODUCTION

Anthony Camacho would like to challenge all sales professionals, entrepreneurs and sales leaders to adapt a power phrase each week and heavily focus on how to implement it within themselves and sales organizations. It's all mindset, what we tell ourselves and how we condition ourselves with our words and thoughts. This book will enhance and empower positive thinking to get greater results in the sales game or that will impact your daily sales activities, increases sales commissions and ultimately these 60 phrases will get you closer to a better lifestyle.

We only have one shot at this life so make it good, count and meaningful. Camacho would also like to encourage all readers of this book to start making notes and writing down their personal and original quotes. Everyone should write at least one book in their life time. Your positive and powerful words are priceless and need to be published for the world to see and legacy continued.

With a purchase of this book and my other published books for your entire sales organization. I will come to give a complimentary sales performance workshop. Email me with your requests.

lachitman@hotmail.com

COMMUNICATION

"A great number of sales leaders think that they are good at communicating, when what they are good at is talking."

"Don't go after complaints, don't go after problems, don't go after blame; GO AFTER THE SALE."

NETWORKING

*"DON'T WAIT FOR OPPORTUN-
ITIES, GET UP AND CREATE THEM,
they are not falling from the sky or
growing on trees."*

*"Don't be comfortable with familiar
faces. EXPAND YOUR NETWORK
and meet new people constantly."*

"CONSTANTLY PUSH OUT OF YOUR COMFORT ZONE, growth and new success is not stagnant in the same place."

"Don't just settle for your back yard and the state you live in SELL WORLD WIDE everyone is a buyer."

TEAM BULDING

"SURROUND YOURSELF WITH GREAT PEOPLE; your income and mental state is dictated by those associations."

"IN ORDER TO LEAD CONNECT you can't do it with a broken sales team."   .

SELLING, SALES, AND PROFITS

"In sales the OPPORTUNITIES and POSSIBILITIES ARE ENDLESS if you are truly looking for them and working them."

"Don't sell yourself short. PRECONCEIVED NOTIONS DESTROY SALES. You don't know 'til you know."

*"THE SALE BEGINS WITH WORK
there is no such thing as a Disneyland
customer tram pulling up to your
office handing out deals."*

*"PREPARE FOR YOUR SALES
SUCCESS and the reward will be
confidence and bigger paychecks."*

"MAKE A STAND AND SELL don't be a player that rides the bench on the sidelines."

"YOUR SALES ARE NO LAUGHING MATTER; it is serious business to be a real sales professional."

"You are in charge of your success, you are in charge of your commission, PUT THE MONEY BALL IN YOUR HANDS stop rolling it away."

"Be willing to do what others are not preparing for, PICK UP YOUR COMPETITIONS COMMISSION all day long."

"When people think of your product, program or service you want them to think of you; GAIN MENTAL MARKET SHARE."

"Don't go after break time, don't go after lunches, don't go after vacations; GO AFTER MONEY MAKING ACTIVITIES."

"It pays better to INCREASE YOUR SALES PERFORMANCE and to decrease your complaints."

"CREATE SALES NOT EXCUSES. I have never seen a sales professional create success or wealth off excuses."

"GREAT LEADERS & SALES PROFESSIONALS DON'T GUESS THEY KNOW THEIR PEOPLES NEEDS, they don't lead or sell blindly in the dark."

"REVIEW YOUR SALES GOALS DAILY, get closer one day at time to the sales results you are striving for."

"*YOU WANT A MONEY TREE FOR CHRISTMAS, LEARN TO SELL and make it Christmas every day.*"

"*The greatest gift you can give to the world and to yourself is to GET PAID DOING WHAT YOU LOVE.*"

"Don't waste your paycheck on guessing customer needs, BET ON KNOWING YOUR CUSTOMER NEEDS and win the sale."

"Get over the sales drought; MAKE IT RAIN WITH SALES and plant referral seeds."

"Today is the day to make that honest decision and look at yourself in the mirror and say SELL OR GO HOME."

"MAKE CUSTOMERS SMILE they won't always remember your name, or remember all that you say. They will always remember how you made them feel."

FOLLOW-UP AND
FOLLOW THROUGH

"BE COURAGEOUS, BOLD AND RELENTLESS when AFTER NEW CLIENTS, there is no room for timidity and fear in the sales game."

"It's not enough to have a great idea, BLUE PRINT YOUR SUCCESS and commit to action."

"We need to be constantly reminded day after day the MONEY IS IN THE FOLLOW UP and in the follow through."

" DON'T FEAR REJECTION; FEAR NOT FOLLOWING UP its like letting dollars slip away from your hands."

"Being talented doesn't make you successful or give you product knowledge. PERSISTENCE LEADS TO SUCCESS."

"You can cash a paycheck, you can cash a money order, but YOU CAN'T CASH EXCUSES."

"SUCCESSFUL SALES PEOPLE FOLLOW UP and make the sale, they are not concerned with rejection and the word no."

"SUCCESSFUL SALES MANAGERS FOLLOW THROUGH, they get involved and don't lead from a far."

COLD CALLING

"ALWAYS BE READY TO CHARGE FORWARD with Cold Calls, Referrals, Presentations and asking for the business."

"NEVER BE AFRAID TO COLD CALL, focus on calling to make new friends and long term business."

"Detach your ego from rejection and negative thoughts; NEVER BE AFRAID TO INTRODUCE YOURSELF and make a cold call."

"CONSTANTLY PUSH OUT OF YOUR COMFORT ZONE, growth and new success is not stagnant in the same place."

"People need to know your name whether or not they do business with you; COLD CALL THE WORLD and make it warm."

"MAKE A STAND AND SELL don't be a player that rides the bench on the sidelines."

WORDS TO LIVE BY IN
SALES AND LIFE

"NOTHING WILL STOP US!"

"Make sure to feel good about your physical, mental and spiritual state. FEEL GOOD TO SELL GREAT and your customers will feel good

"You are not a victim of circumstance; BE THE SCULPTOR OF YOUR SUCCESS and start chiseling away."

"Include the balance of working hard and playing hard in your personal and professional life style."

"There is an abundance of doors that lead to opportunities; NEVER BE AFRAID TO DOOR KNOCK and walk in."

"Don't just build a career and an ordinary life, BUILD YOUR EMPIRE and leave a legacy."

"Just because the weather is gloomy and your environment is too, remember YOU CREATE THE SUNNY DAYS in every area of your life."

"There are no easy short cuts on your way to the top; GO AFTER SUCCESS ONE STEP AT A TIME."

"THOUGHTS CAN MOVE THE UNIVERSE what you see in your mind's eye will manifest into existence."

"THE BEST INVESTMENT IN LIFE IS TIME WELL SPENT and not wasting it on non-productive activities."

"Build friendships... PEOPLE NEED TO KNOW YOUR NAME whether they are doing business with you or not."

"There are 24 hours in a day DON'T LET ONE BAD HOUR RUIN THE WEEK OR THE MONTH; focus on the next hour to be the changer."

"CHEERS FOR TAKING ACTION TOWARD YOUR SUCCESS; that is something worth celebrating looking back on your life."

"CREATE THE LIFE STYLE YOU WANT don't let a person, place or thing take away the life you want."

"SUIT UP FOR YOUR SUCCESS if you want people to take you seriously you have to take yourself seriously."

"SUCCESS IS ONLY ONE WAY UP you can't be looking for it on the bottom."

"GREAT LEADERS & SALES PROFESSIONALS POSSESS THE POWER OF INFLUENCE they don't just manage a lifeless process."

"INVEST IN YOUR PROFESSIONAL DEVELOPMENT. Your mind is the greatest return on investment."

ABOUT THE AUTHOR

Anthony Camacho also known as the HITMAN is an International Sales Performance Trainer, multi published author and a bestselling author as well. He attributes his selling success to his love of people. He has invested tens of thousands of dollars in books, workshops and seminars to understand human behavior, leadership and influence in order to best serve his clients.

Camacho has in-person cold called millions of dollars in sales through his skill-set of making friends and connecting with people. He was known in his former company as "The Hitman" for his high-closing, new accounts ratio. Now he spends 100% of his time teaching sales professionals, entrepreneurs and multi-million dollar companies how to do the same.

In 2013, at the top of his selling career, he opened his own business as a motivational speaker and sales trainer. His goal is to change the world view of salesmanship both inside and outside of the sales industry.

To expand what you learn in Anthony's Itty Bitty Book, you can attend his live events, request a workshop, and visit his website at:
http://www.topproducerfactory.com

If you enjoyed this Itty Bitty® book you might also enjoy...

- Your Amazing Itty Bitty® Little Black Book of Sales by Anthony Camacho

- Your Amazing Itty Bitty® Little Black Book of Success for Sales Leaders by Anthony Camacho

Coming Soon

- Your Amazing Itty Bitty® Little Black Book of Successful In Person Cold Calling by Anthony Camacho

- Your Amazing Itty Bitty® Little Black Book of Sales Mastery by Anthony Camacho

Or any of our other Itty Bitty® books available online at http://www.ittybittypublishing.com/.

Made in the USA
Las Vegas, NV
07 October 2021